Su Dongpo

CHINESE GENIUS

DEMI

LEE & LOW BOOKS INC.

NEW YORK

SOURCES

Clark, Cyril Drummond Le Gros. *Selections from Su Tung-po*. London: Jonathan Cape and Harrison Smith, 1931.

Grant, Beata. *Mount Lu Revisited: Buddhism in the Life and Writings of Su Shih*. Honolulu: University of Hawaii Press, 1994.

Su Dongpo. *Selected Poems of Su Tung-p'o*. Translated by Burton Watson. Port Townsend, WA: Copper Canyon Press, 1994.

Wayley, Arthur. *The Way and Its Power: Lao Tzu's Tao Te Ching and Its Place in Chinese Thought*. New York: Grove Press, 1958.

Wilhelm, Richard. *The I Ching or Book of Changes*. Bollingen Series XIX. Princeton: Princeton University Press, 1950.

Yuan-Zhong, Xu. *Su Dong-po: A New Translation*. Hong Kong: The Commercial Press, 1982.

Yutang, Lin. *The Gay Genius: The Life and Times of Su Tungpo*. New York: John Day Company, 1947.

Some variations may exist in transliterations of Chinese words, names, and geographical locations. This book uses the Pinyin system of romanization, except when referring to *Taoism* and the *Tao Te Ching*, which are commonly recognized terms in the English language.

On the cover and title page, the Chinese calligraphy is Su Dongpo's signature as it was appended to a poem in 1084. It is translated as "Written by Shih, the Layman of Eastern Slope."

Manufactured in China
Book production by The Kids at Our House

The text is set in Tiepolo
The illustrations are rendered in paint and ink
Calligraphy by Jeanyee Wong
Book design by Michael Nelson

10 9 8 7 6 5 4 3 2 1
First Edition

LIBRARY OF CONGRESS CATALOGING-IN-PUBLICATION DATA
Demi.
Su Dongpo : Chinese genius / by Demi.—1st ed.   p. cm.
Summary: "A biography of Su Dongpo, Chinese poet, civil engineer, and statesman,
whose appreciation for nature and justice were evident in his works
and led him to experience both triumph and adversity
in 11th century China"—Provided by publisher.
ISBN-13: 978-1-58430-256-8   ISBN-10: 1-58430-256-9
1. Su, Shih, 1037–1101—Juvenile literature. 2. Authors, Chinese—Biography—Juvenile literature. I. Title.
PL2685.Z5D46 2006
895.1'84209—dc22
2005030437

In loving memory of Karen Chinn—

wife, mother, and author

YELLOW SEA

EAST CHINA SEA

SOUTH CHINA SEA

Yellow River

Yangtze River

KAIFENG

FENGXIANG

MEISHAN

HUANGZHOU

SUZHOU

HUZHOU

HANGZHOU

GUANGZHOU

HAINAN ISLAND

SU DONGPO'S CHINA 1036-1101

SU DONGPO
(1036–1101)

When people of China hear the name Su Dongpo, they smile, for he is at the heart and soul of Chinese culture. His life embodied the enlightenment of Buddhism, the simplicity of Taoism, and the wise teachings of Confucianism. He was also China's knight-errant, traveling the country and helping others with true generosity of spirit.

Many say Su Dongpo was China's greatest genius. He was a statesman, philosopher, poet, painter, engineer, architect, and humanitarian who approached everything with joy and grace. He created masterful works of poetry and art that were renowned in his lifetime and revered centuries later. All the while Su Dongpo lead an exemplary life of public duty as a leader, scholar, and judge. He created China's first public hospital, invented sanitation systems, improved the welfare of prisoners, standardized grain prices, granted college loans, worked for the relief of famine victims, fought government corruption, and reconstructed West Lake in Hangzhou to the paradise it is today.

So significant and far-reaching was the scope of Su Dongpo's lifeworks that they appear almost superhuman, as does the man himself. Perhaps Su Dongpo's greatest legacy of all was the example he set with his indomitable spirit. It shone like a star through life's triumphs and adversity and lives on in eternity.

—Demi

AT THE FOOT OF OMEI SHAN,
the highest mountain in all of China,
in the little village of Meishan, Sichuan,
a boy named Su Shih was born.

"There was in him a force of character that
could not be stopped by anyone,
a force that started at the moment of his birth."
—Lin Yutang

His family were scholars, and his mother taught Su Shih and his younger brother, Su Ziyou, simple classic stories and the value of study. She told her son, "As a little seed one day will become a great tree, as a flowing river can carve a mighty rock, neither of these can you see at work with your own eyes. But one day their effort will show! One day the work you do will show too!"

Su Shih's mother taught her children that all living things, no matter how small, possessed *qi*, the force of life itself, and were to be treated with love and care. Because Su Shih lived in harmony with nature, the smallest birds felt safe to land in his hand.

Often Su Shih helped his mother in the vegetable garden. One day he dug up an ancient and very precious inkstone. This was a lucky omen foretelling greatness, as an inkstone was one of the four treasures of great men, along with the ink, the brush, and the silk.

At age six, with his new treasure, Su Shih began writing short stories. With rapid strokes as fast as the wind, he made his brush dance on paper!

"He used his pen as if it were a toy; his words were as spontaneous as a bird's song in spring; a cricket's chirp in autumn; and the storks in high heaven unaware of human listeners below!"

—Ouyang Xiu

At age eleven Su Shih entered secondary school in preparation for the official exams. Su Shih read all the ancient classics, history, poetry, and prose. These works had to be recited in class with his back to the teacher so Su Shih couldn't see the open textbook.

Su Shih copied and recopied the classics word for word. He learned each book so deeply, in such a way that no amount of reading alone would have given him.

This practice with the Chinese paintbrush made his calligraphy superb, and he developed mystical painting skills. His painting was an act of magic. He could produce wonderful effects through mastery of the secret forces in nature.

Practicing for the official exams, Su Shih and his brother, Su Ziyou, recited the classics for hours while their father lay on the couch and corrected even the slightest error in pronunciation.

Soon many people came out just to listen. The sound of the brothers' voices was said to be the most musical upon the earth, in tune with nature like the flowing of water.

The brothers were so close and played with words so freely, they could write poems to each other that could be read forward and backward and even in a circle!

One poem compared the human spirit to a flying bird:

To what can human life be likened?
Perhaps to a wild goose's footprint on snow;
The foot's imprint is accidentally left,
But carefree, the bird flies east and west.

In 1056 when Su Shih was twenty, his father thought both of his sons were ready for the official exams. For two months they traveled north through the mountain ranges of Sichuan and Shenxi before arriving at Kaifeng, the great capital.

Ouyang Xiu, the First Writer of the land, was nominated by Emperor Renzong to be chief examiner. Candidates had to come to the palace at dawn, bringing their cold meals with them. Then they were shut up in cubicles under the supervision of palace guards for two days.

Su Ziyou passed with high honors, but Su Shih was decorated *jinshi*—the head of all successful candidates! This honor meant that instantly Su Shih became known as the First Scholar in all the land!

Emperor Jentsung announced, "The Su brothers are my two future premiers!"

Now that they were guaranteed official careers, the brothers set up households in the capital, and all were joyous.

But amid this happiness came news of their mother's sudden death. The family returned home to mourn.

Eulogizing his mother in heaven,
Su Shih wrote:

*Water flows on and on
but it never flows away.
The moon waxes and wanes,
and yet in the end it is the same moon.
If we look at things through the eyes
    of change,
then there's not a single instant of stillness
    in all creation.
But if we observe the changelessness
    of things,
then we, and all beings alike
have no end.*

After twenty-seven months of mourning, father and sons returned to Kaifeng by boat on the powerful and treacherous Yangtze River. Before entering the most dangerous gorges, everyone prayed to the gods for protection. Su Shih and Su Ziyou, exhilarated by what they saw, wrote more than one hundred verses along the way!

Su Shih wrote:

*Entering the gorge, the river seemed blocked
    in front.
Then suddenly the cliffs opened as if by the
    power of heaven.
The swirling waters began to leave their
    wide expanse
And narrow themselves into a deep abyss,
The winds bellowed through the cliffs,
And clouds spewed forth from the caves.
Overhanging cliffs whistled in the high winds,
And twining vines glistened in resplendent
    green.
Bamboo groves stood over rocks, dripping
    with cold verdure,
And rhododendrons dotted the mountainside.
Falling cataracts spread a shower of
    snowy mist,
And strange rocks sped past like horses
    in fright.*

Su Shih himself felt like the force of
water—ready to conquer the world.

Su Shih's first position was as assistant magistrate in Fengxiang—in far western China. He brilliantly organized the timber transportation for the building of Emperor Jentsung's tomb. He chose the perfect pillars of pine for the ancestral hall. The pillars were considered symbols of fortitude, self-discipline, and greatness, and ensured eternal life.

In times of drought Su Shih prayed
to the Heavenly Dragon God for rain,
and he was so successful at bringing rain,
he was considered a god himself.

Su Shih traveled all over Fengxiang
Province as judge, settling legal cases
fairly. Just as Su Shih's writing followed
the laws of nature, so did his rulings,
which were just and as brilliant as the
sun. He was guided by the ancient
Chinese book of wisdom, the *Tao Te
Ching*, which says:

The wise man teaches without words,
Governs without making claims,
and controls without making pressure,
and so everyone will flourish.
                    —*Tao Te Ching*, Chapter II

One rainy day a poor fan seller accused of many debts was brought before Su Shih. The poor fan seller said, "It isn't that I don't want to pay my debts, but it has rained so heavily—nobody needs fans!"

Su Shih told the man to lay out all his fans on the table before him. Then Su Shih began painting and writing poetry like a whirlwind on the hundreds of fans. Giving them back to the poor man, Su Shih said, "Now go out, sell these, and pay your debts!"

For his just rulings and noble deeds, Su Shih was considered a great humanitarian and friend of all the people.

Soon Su Shih was appointed secretary in the Department of History, and magistrate of the metropolis. But now he encountered a great power struggle. His rival, Wang Anshi, a self-righteous man, had been appointed premier by the new emperor, Shenzong.

Emperor Shenzong wanted quick and sweeping social reforms to ensure his own success and instant glory. Wang Anshi wanted success and instant glory too.

Su Shih knew that sudden and badly planned reforms would not solve anything. He predicted disaster, and disaster occurred. Without capable men to implement Wang Anshi's reforms, chaos and corruption resulted. Floods and famine spread throughout the land.

Peasants fled their homes to avoid paying Wang Anshi's reform tax and being jailed!

With his forceful character, Su Shih could not refrain from writing poems of protest. He told his brother: "When I find something is wrong, it is like finding a fly in my food, and I just have to spit it out."

In his poems, he denounced bad government, saying it was the same as robbery "in God's eyes!" He compared corrupt officials to croaking frogs, chirping cicadas, hooting owls, black crows feeding on rotten mice, and monkeys dressed up in coats and hats!

Su Shih's poems were instantly popular and were recited throughout the land. Wang Anshi was furious and wanted Su Shih out of sight. Su Shih was moved as magistrate to Hangzhou, then to Mizhou, then to Huzhou, then to Suzhou.

In Suzhou, Wang Anshi's dredging of the Yellow River for better commerce had failed. The river had overflowed its banks and flooded the city. Su Shih was left to pick up the pieces.

And pick up the pieces he did. Living in a shack on top of the city wall, Su Shih directed all works to stop the flooding. Splashing about in the mud, he personally stopped people from leaving the city and got them to help.

Su Shih's defense works held, the flood subsided, and Su Shih was a hero! He built the Great Yellow Tower overlooking the city as a symbol of what people can do when they work together.

Su Shih's success was too much for Wang Anshi to bear. He incited the First Persecution of Scholars for persons disrespectful of the government. Su Shih was arrested, condemned, demoted, and banished south to Huangzhou on the Yangtze River.

Lucky to be alive, Su Shih felt like a feather torn apart in a whirlwind. He became quiet and meditative. He began to forget distinctions between fame and obscurity, riches and poverty, intelligence and stupidity, pride and humility, jealousy and compassion. He began to forget himself. And he began to experience great happiness and enlightenment.

Now Su Shih could find beauty anywhere. With magnificent mountains and changing, misty clouds, Huangzhou was more like heaven than Earth. With all of nature's beauty spread before him, Su Shih began a new life of being unknown.

Su Shih became a farmer on the Eastern slope, or *Dongpo*, and from then on he was called Su Dongpo. He was very poor. He planted rice, wheat, and vegetables, tea fields and mulberry bushes, and a great orchard of orange and persimmon trees. Peasants and farmers befriended him. Even hermit monks who had spent all their lives in towering mountain caves came to see him.

"Blessed are those who are deprived of all the 'good' things on Earth!" Su Dongpo said happily.

In his new state of enchanted living, Su Dongpo did some of his best writing, including his first poem about visiting the Red Cliff on the Yangtze River:

Letting the boat go where it pleased,
we drifted over the immeasurable fields
   of water.
I felt a boundless exhilaration,
as though I were sailing on a void
or riding the wind
and didn't know where to stop.
I was filled with a lightness,
As though I had left the world
and were standing alone, or had
   sprouted wings
and were flying up to join the immortals!

In 1084 news came that Su Dongpo was pardoned and wanted back in service by Emperor Shenzong. From his sublime peace, Su Dongpo had no desire for worldly fame. He tried to say no, but the emperor insisted.

On his departure, the entire village followed Su Dongpo as far as they could on donkeys and horses and in little boats, to say farewell.

Before Su Dongpo reached the capital, Emperor Shenzong died, and the Grand Empress Dowager Gao became ruling regent for the boy emperor, Zhezong. Now Su Dongpo, at age forty-nine, was catapulted into the highest position of power. He was appointed secretary to the emperor and was to write and issue edicts with the empress!

With great ceremony and fanfare, Su Dongpo was given an official jacket with a gold belt, and a magnificent white horse. He was at the height of fame—the favorite of the empress, the First Scholar of the land, and the admired sage who had suffered for his wisdom.

But Su Dongpo said:

There is not much difference in the actual
    happiness
of living a luxurious life and a simple one.
One is wanted for position
When one doesn't want it, and wants it
when the position doesn't want him.
In either case, happiness and sadness
are moments that pass like a shadow,
a sound, a breeze and a dream.
Both are earthly illusions.
How can one find happiness
Countering one illusion with another?

Again Su Dongpo was envied by his old enemies and was accused of being disrespectful to the government.
    The empress ignored these charges, but like "humming mosquitoes" they continued. Finally, Su Dongpo requested that he be allowed to return to a life of peace. The empress understood and honored him with the position of governor of his beloved Huangzhou.

In 1093 the empress dowager died. The eighteen-year-old Zhezong became emperor. He had spent his years not with the classics, but with wine, women, and song. Being ignorant and weak, he allowed corruption and evil to flourish. The Second Persecution of Scholars began. All learned men were degraded, humiliated, and exiled to Guangzhou.

Su Dongpo began the long march of 1500 miles from Huangzhou to Guangzhou. On the way he learned he had been demoted a second rank, then a third, then a fourth—from commander and governor, to minister and magistrate, to nobody.

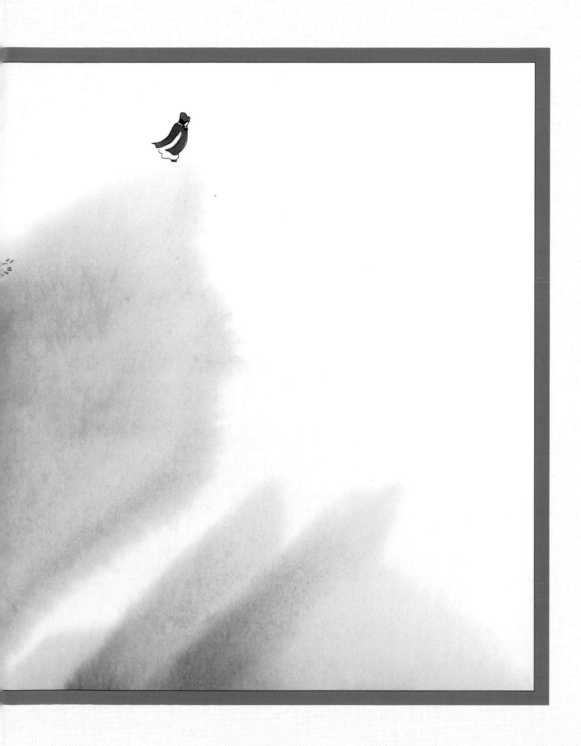

Coming through the mountain pass
near the end of his journey, Su Dongpo
stood on a mountain peak so close
to the clouds and sky that he felt a
part of them and that his life was
a living dream.

Eventually Su Dongpo was exiled outside of China to Hainan Island, a place inhabited only by natives. Su Dongpo was sixty and never thought he would see China again. His beloved brother, Su Ziyou, who had been banished to Guangzhou, saw Su Dongpo off in a little boat. Even then they could not refrain from writing poems to each other. For the brothers whose words and voices once blended like flowing water, this would be their last meeting on Earth.

In Hainan, Su Dongpo's roof on his shabby little hut leaked so much that he had to move his bed from one place to another at night. This was real exile! No food was available. He ate cockleburs and nettles and "rays of the morning sun!"

Su Dongpo wrote:

The climate of Hainan is damp
and a humid swampy atmosphere
rises from the ground rotting everything.
How can a human being stand this for long?
But a lot of life depends on merely adjusting
    to surroundings:
a salamander can live in fire;
and silkworm eggs can be preserved on ice.
By mental control, I shut off my mind
and turn on my spirit!

And with his indomitable spirit,
Su Dongpo kept his joy for living.
Knowing fortune and adversity to be
two sides of a single truth gave him
peace. He was able to forgive his
enemies, saying, "In my mind there is
not a single bad man in all the world!"
    Free at last, Su Dongpo returned to
his love of writing. He made his own
paper and brushes—and nearly burned
down his hut making ink! He wrote
his *Allegories, Book of Journals, Book of
History,* and *Echoing Poems.*

In this simple happiness, news came to Su Dongpo that he was pardoned once again. Emperor Zhezong had died at age twenty-four.

Su Dongpo had another triumphal return! In every town he was greeted and cheered. He was decorated and celebrated. Thousands of people crowded the riverbanks and highways just to see him pass.

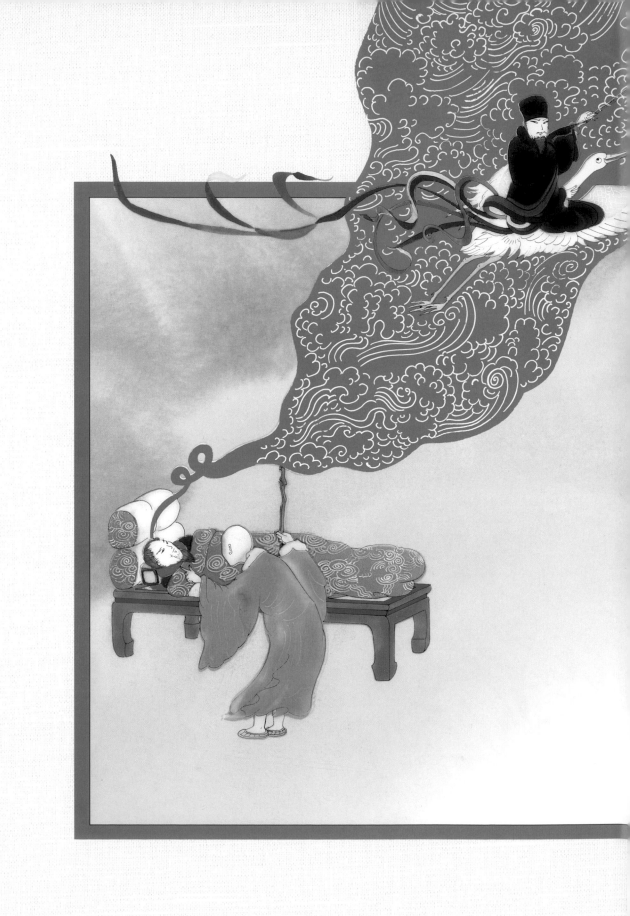

In the midst of all these celebrations, Su Dongpo suddenly fell ill, and no amount of medicine could cure him. Rapidly his condition worsened. A worried monk near to him said, "At this moment try to think of the life hereafter." Su Dongpo replied peacefully, "The hereafter does exist, but trying to get there won't help, for salvation consists in being naturally and unconsciously good."

Su Dongpo shut his eyes and joined eternity.

He was,
The Very Best

The very best is like water
That benefits all things without trying to;
That is content with low places that others dislike.
That is why water is so near to Heaven's Way.
The very best in their homes love simplicity;
In their hearts love what is deep;
In their words love what is true.
In friendship love what is gentle.
In their world love what is peaceful,
In government love what is orderly,
In deeds love what is right,
In actions love what is timely.

It is because they do not compete
with others
That they are loved by all.
          —*Tao Te Ching*, Chapter VIII